INDUSTRY &
THE COAST

INDUSTRY & THE COAST

IMAGES OF THE NORTH EAST IN THE 1960s

RICHARD GAUNT

FONTHILL

Fonthill Media Limited
Fonthill Media LLC
www.fonthillmedia.com
office@fonthillmedia.com

First published in the United Kingdom 2015

British Library Cataloguing in Publication Data:
A catalogue record for this book is available from the British Library

ISBN 978-1-78155-256-8

Typeset in 10.5pt on 13pt Sabon
Printed and bound in England

Contents

1

The North East in the 1960s

I took a lot of photographs of different places around the North East of England in the 1960s. First, it was mainly the steam locomotives which were more or less everywhere you went on the railways at the beginning of the decade, though they had all gone from British Railways lines by 1968.[1] But increasingly I gathered images of lots of other things I came across in everyday life: a sort of diary in pictures, if you like. Other people write about what happens to them in notebooks; for whatever reason, I found myself doing something similar, but taking pictures of what I saw with black and white film.

The years went by and I looked at some of these images every so often. Nostalgia is powerful stuff and occasionally I'd enjoy warm feelings looking back through these images of places and times I'd nearly forgotten. Mostly, though, the negatives sat in envelopes in boxes which lay untouched in our attic. In all honesty, they were lucky to survive various house moves, and could very easily have ended up in landfill.

At the time I took the photographs, I had no real sense of history-in-the-making, nor what was to come more generally. I knew that there were concerns about jobs—and indeed whole industries—and it was easy to work out that some familiar sights might not be around forever. But the idea that the time might not come when there would be no deep mines, nor working shipyards, nor much in the way of heavy industry at all, never occurred to me. For the North East has been hit by wave after wave of change—not all bad, but much of it very painful indeed for communities. Before too long, photographs of what had once been commonplace just couldn't be taken any more.

Moving on nearly half a century, I started having discussions with Alan Sutton and his colleagues about producing books using some of these images—first the steam engine pictures, then the scenes of more general daily life in the North East as it used to be.

The obvious angle to concentrate on was all the changes which hit the region during the 1960s and afterwards, but this was not enough to give a structure for ordering the various images and the text to describe them. The North East is now, and was in the 1960s, a complex place. The stereotypes suggest a lot of industry, but it is equally home to charming villages, market towns, and rugged moorland.

Above: Changes in musical taste and fashions: often home-grown, but still looking with admiration across the Atlantic. Here, Roy Orbison hits town.

Below: Different kinds of change, like attitudes to playing in the street (less and less of a good idea as rising prosperity brought more motorcars).

An area where heavy industry was prone to dominate the skyline and the job market. I found it wonderfully dramatic to photograph, but with hindsight maybe tended to over-emphasise the blacker, smokier tones (not that working in pastel shades was really an option).

Bit by bit, the shape of two books emerged with a rough East/West split—the first looking at the area to the West including Darlington and Durham, and this book concentrating on the coast and the more industrial areas to the East. This seemed to make sense not only in the split of the areas, but for a lot of the subject matter too: obviously enough, the various ports and harbours are only looked at in this book; the Pennines are only in the book on the West.

Now these are no textbooks or systematic surveys of the region. Some parts are covered better than others; some, I am sorry to say, aren't covered at all. I lived in Darlington at the time these photographs were taken, so I tend to have more material for South Durham and North Yorkshire, but that's not always the case: Seaham Harbour, for example, seemed to get a lot of coverage.

Within this uneven framework I haven't felt the need to be bound by official boundaries, which in any case were becoming blurred even in the 1960s. The emergence of Teesside as a separate municipal entity significantly altered the official distinction between what had previously been Yorkshire and Durham.

Plenty of stereotypical views if you wanted them—like terraced housing, lots of it, close to where people worked. Change has remained the dominant starting point for picking out particular images and writing a few words prompted by them. But you have to be careful. Most lifetimes see many things changing; it seems to be a fundamental part of the human condition.

The North Sea gives one important example of change—its name, no longer the 'German Ocean' as relations between Britain and Germany deteriorated and the Great War approached. Whatever you call it, it has exerted a powerful influence over the region: always there, though variable in mood and the way men used it. During the 1960s, there was fishing, shipping coal to market, tipping mine waste … even occasional swimming. Dotted along the coast: sea stacks, interesting little coves, and other features. Many are starting to look really attractive in a conventional, tourist-friendly way again, now that the natural stone is back from beneath the industrial overlay.

Above and below: The state of the beaches varied a lot in the 1960s: from attractive golden sands to the roughest kinds of industrial debris. I want to be fair to the authorities who obviously knew about the offshore currents and could keep black mine waste and other rubbish away from the sands if they wanted to. It had to go somewhere, and other places weren't quite so pretty. The abandoned doll glares out: just another piece of plastic jetsam or something more sinister?

Potentially this could have been highly contentious because of the Yorkshire boundary's importance for cricketers' eligibility to play for the White Rose County—though less so now. But there was a ready-to-go solution for coping with these boundary changes close to hand for cricketing purposes: ignore them!

Further north, the distinction between Durham and Northumberland was also becoming less clear through processes which were to lead to the formation of Tyne & Wear County Council in 1974 and the Metro transit system in 1980.

While most images are clearly from the 1960s, I have been flexible here too, and included a couple of more recent photographs which seemed to be relevant.

The subject of this book, the East of the region, is where most people live and where the majority of the factories and pits are (or rather, were) close to the mouths of the Tees, Tyne, and Wear. There are, obviously enough, substantial areas of farmland and some pretty towns and villages. But if you really want tranquil, rural surroundings, you may well have come to the wrong place, and might like to think of heading west.

In the 1960s, the coal industry was what linked the East and West of the area, having been mined from beneath most of County Durham and a good part of Northumberland at various times. But closer to the coast there were—at least in the 1960s—hosts of heavy engineering, iron, steel, chemicals, and shipbuilding activities, which dominated the skyline and the job market in about equal measure.

I suppose there are different kinds of change. These areas have a long history, seeing changes to almost every aspect of life, landscape, and belief. The sea has been one constant, but the way human beings have used it has changed wildly over the centuries.

It is easy to think of the North Sea solely as a place where fishermen make their living and commercial shipping plods to and fro. But let's not forget that, in Britain at least, the name change away from the German Ocean is only about a hundred years old. There have been plenty more changes too: around a thousand years before this book was even thought of, the German Ocean (or North Sea) brought the Viking raiders, who generated significant changes to the way things were organised and funded in the region. They did so in, of course, in their own special way—although lately they seem to have been getting some sort of reputational makeover, which plays down their 'bloodthirsty savage' dimension and encourages increased attention to their skills as navigators and metalworkers.

Long-term changes of a different kind have come to places like Jarrow and Monkwearmouth. Nowadays, these are relatively small communities within the greater Tyneside and Wearside conurbations respectively, but the Jarrow hunger marches, which pricked many consciences about poverty in the industrial areas of Britain in the great depression, are still within living memory (just) and many people in the 1960s would remember them well. And if we scroll back to the times of the Venerable Bede, these were major monastic centres, whose fame must have reached across the whole of the known world.

All of this is designed to put change in the 1960s in the North East into some sort of context. These were areas which have seen a lot of change in the past, and there is no obvious sign of it ending.

Heavy industry going strong, at least for the time being: for the passing photographer, great shapes and outlines. I sometimes waited until there was a figure in the viewfinder to give a bit of scale and added interest. It usually did not make a lot of difference; such was the scale of the operations all around that it might not be easy to spot a human being at all. Yet this was no spirit-crushing environment for the people who worked there, who told you about good pay and plenty of support from your mates.

Strong sunlight on a winter's afternoon brought yet further dimensions of visual drama. I thought it was wonderful, but the public mood seemed to be getting less sympathetic. The impact on the landscape was becoming a bit unfashionable, and attention to 'the environment' growing all the time. Together with growing evidence that organisations in Germany and Japan were making things more accurately, quickly, and sometimes at lower prices, great traditions turned into constraints rather than sources of strength and pride.

Change came to churches too. This is St Andrew's Presbyterian at Hebburn, latterly the subject of many hopes and plans, including conversion into a brewery.

Right and below: Changing attitudes to gambling and games of chance. But these were still heavily regulated: Redcar was not going to challenge Las Vegas in the foreseeable future. Constructing the beehive hairstyle called for a whole load of structural engineering skills (at least so I was told), but not of the sort the area had long been famous for.

Changes in attitude and cultures are harder to run with than declining economic competitiveness. How important were the arrival of the miniskirt and international pop culture? Maybe the answer is that in themselves they didn't mean very much for the long term, but perhaps they were symptoms of something else, which probably was more significant. Looking back, there was certainly a lot of *talk* about change in the 1960s—particularly in popular music, and what young people wore and how they behaved. Eric Burdon, The Animals, the polo neck sweater, Chelsea boots, and the occasional Afghan coat went along with new(ish) attitudes to what was within reach in terms of careers, beliefs, and relationships.

As ever, some people liked the changes they were seeing, and may even have described them as 'groovy' at the time. Others, whose traditional values were under threat, didn't like what they were seeing at all, namely the 'permissive' changes in regulations and attitudes to subjects as varied as gambling, hire purchase, and teenage pregnancy.

I think it's fair to say that in the 1960s, older people talked quite a bit about changes they thought they were seeing in the ways younger people were thinking and behaving—maybe with more emphasis on the individual and rights, and less on communities and responsibilities. Certainly, a lot of people growing up in the 1960s took more of an interest in what they wore, liked very different kinds of music, and seemed to have a rather more relaxed attitude to authority than their parents.

But everyone tended to be a bit more prosperous, too, which made an interest in fashion, vinyl records, and consumer durables a whole lot easier.

What did any of this mean for someone with a camera and a bit of curiosity in and around Teesside, Wearside, and Tyneside? Visually, a lot still hinged on the traditional heavy industries. In much of the area, you couldn't go far without seeing a pithead and some spoil heaps. The Tyneside skyline had an army of shipyard cranes; taking the train from Middlesbrough to Saltburn brought passengers almost within touching distance of several miles of smoking furnaces and factories. Most passengers took no notice, of course, but it was high drama for me, and sometimes my camera.

A lot of the industrial problems had been there for many decades without leading to terminal decline, but anyone who listened to the radio or read the papers could see that these mighty industrial enterprises might not be there forever. This did not go unnoticed in faraway Whitehall; indeed the Cabinet had a Minister for the North East for a while, and long-forgotten initiatives like the Selective Employment Tax were designed to improve the competitiveness of this and other 'depressed' regions, like Clydeside and the South Wales valleys. Fine new roads were built and there were other investments in 'infrastructure', like the vast Kielder and Cow Green reservoirs high up in the hills, which make it difficult to envisage a time when taps in the area are ever going to run dry.

Yet investments in infrastructure—like various other interventions to promote business growth—did not seem to make much long-term difference. Cruelly, the industries in the North East were often inter-linked, so problems for one were felt at further stages in the supply chain. Shipbuilding takes a lot of steel, and a new mill making plate was installed at Consett as late as 1961, expecting to send a lot of product to shipyards on the Tyne and Wear. North-eastern yards were world-leading for many years, but ship-owners had already started to go to other yards across the globe which were simply making them better offers.

One way or another, the area saw a wholesale slaughter of much of its heavy engineering, and not just in the 1960s. By the 1980s, Mrs Thatcher was able to take her 'Walk in the Wilderness' and posed for photographers on the site of the once-mighty Head Wrightson factory in Stockton. The coal industry has gone too … I could go on.

It is probably true to say that a lot of what was happening here was happening in other parts of Britain too. But maybe it was a bit more extreme in the North East. One way or another, it seemed to me that if I wanted to photograph any scenes of the heavy industry which had been so familiar for decades, I'd better get going.

When this heavy industry was in full production, what we now regard as pollution was normally not far behind. This was a particular feature of Teesside, with chemical plants and steel works—and a lot of them. That meant a lot of general haze in the air, which had pros and cons in photographic terms. Mostly it was a nuisance: reduced clarity and contrast flattened a lot of details and led to general dullness and drear. It wasn't always bad, though, and if you were careful and lucky, the haze might even work for you by giving a bit of perspective and depth. Not natural territory for a latter-day Canaletto, maybe; I am not so sure about Turner.

A lot of heavy industry cries out for dramatic pictures of big, bold, black surfaces, maybe with some billowing white steam clouds to add contrast. Depending on your point of view, however, the overall impression can be a bit gloomy, and maybe a bit menacing or overpowering.

I don't want to make too many apologies: when I got to spend time in some of these plants, they were just as exciting and awe-inspiring as I had imagined from the outside. It's possible to lighten things up considerably while processing individual images, but it seems to me that this doesn't do justice to the flames and the darkness, and the sheer bulk of what was really there. That's just the way it is when you're working on the coke ovens or a big machine is bashing metal in an echoing fabrication shop.

There was, of course, a more relaxed attitude to pollution generally: all sorts of things went into the atmosphere or the North Sea. Burning and tipping faced a fraction of the regulations we have today.

But that's probably enough quibbling. By no means the whole of the area depended on declining heavy industry in the 1960s; chemicals and petrochemicals were still expanding; pretty towns and villages like Sedgefield dated back to well before the Industrial Revolution; and the New Towns of Washington and Peterlee stressed that they were not going to be perpetuating the heavy engineering and mining heritage which surrounded them.

I have to admit that back in the 1960s, I did not take a lot of notice of the New Towns, maybe because they did not seem to be 'threatened' in any way. I took very few photographs of them at all, and even this handful tended to point to a general lack of interest on my part.

Shipyard cranes on a misty Tyneside day: less and less work about, either for building or repairing vessels. The shipbuilding industry didn't suddenly disappear: modernising investments were made, small firms merged into larger ones, worthy reports were written. But before long, once-busy yards fell silent.

Vickers Armstrong was a mighty name on Tyneside for decades. This image would fit into a message about industrial decline in the North East nicely, but there is, I'm afraid, something of a problem: I took the photograph in Barrow-in-Furness. Maybe the message is still valid, however.

Atmospheric pollution was normally a downright nuisance to a photographer, destroying shadows and contrast. You could be lucky: if the persistent haze was thinned by wind or rain, there might be just enough to give perspective and character to the rooftops, chimneys, and spires of the industrial landscape beneath the Transporter Bridge across the Tees.

It was not difficult to spot why the atmosphere looked hazy most of the time. Big chimneys were busy shifting largely untreated smoke and fumes in great volume. Less easy to spot from a distance was the contribution made by grit and debris flying off tips of coke, coal, sand, various ores, and the rest—but it was clear enough if you walked past on a windy day.

Pollution wasn't simply atmospheric: the attraction of the North Sea as a way of getting rid of all sorts of unwanted substances seemed irresistible. Yet this was no conspiracy (at least, as far as I know it wasn't). There was simply a more relaxed approach to what we'd now immediately attack as irresponsible and mindless pollution.

Above and right: Not too far away from some serious manufacturing capacity: pantiled roofing along the coast in picturesque Whitby, and the quiet backstreets of Yarm (with the railway viaduct behind).

Above and below: Links between industry and nearby rural areas ran two ways: untold tons of limestone has left North Yorkshire for the Teesside furnaces. In return, while these ex-North Eastern Railway coaches might have been designed originally for railway purposes only, many years later, when that job was done, deep in the countryside they were given an attractive new career opportunity—providing shelter for chickens.

The traditional face of mining: steel girders for the head frame, exposed winding wheels—at worst, the backdrop to grim, nerve-shredding scenes when something had gone wrong underground. Here it is all much sunnier, as a 'Lambton tank' sets out with yet more coal to be exported from the staithes (referred to locally as 'drops') at Sunderland. If you look closely, you can see that the scene is a bit misleading: there are no cables in the headgear, and this shaft—like many others—has only been kept open for ventilation and rescue purposes.

Including the rural areas, particularly in North Yorkshire, gives some balance to all that heavy industry, and reminds us of more human-scale living and working environments not too far away. As an aside, it has always seemed to me that villages like Staithes (on the way to Whitby) are just as attractive as anything in Cornwall. Going north, the glorious beaches of Northumberland are dramatic in a different way, but you have to wait till you get well beyond Blyth for the best of them.

Economically, the industrial and rural areas were often linked of course; a lot of the early development of the ironworks on Teesside depended on ore from the Cleveland hills in North Yorkshire, and blast furnaces still depend on trainloads of local limestone to feed them to this day.

I've already mentioned the role of coal for many generations—providing plenty of mining jobs for many years—but there were also jobs in coking plants, by-product factories, transport, and the rest. Meeting requirements for transporting high-quality coal from the easily seams in the west was where the Stockton and Darlington Railway and the others came in, building on what had been learned on much older tramways and waggonways, and technological innovation from the banks of the Tyne and elsewhere. That gave us the steam locomotive, the standard gauge, and all the rest of it. Ports in the estuaries and along the Durham coast did very nicely too.

In the 1960s, the Coal Board was still actively recruiting, using a slogan along the lines of, 'There will always be a future for a bright lad in Britain's modern mining industry.' I've written elsewhere about how I and a busload of other teenagers took advantage of these recruitment plans and had a couple of days out experiencing the mining industry at first hand. Unfortunately for the NCB, few, if any, of us signed up—not least because of the advice from a couple of the pitmen we met, 'to work anywhere in the world apart from doon the pit.'

I need to say a bit more about how these photographs came to be taken. I've written in other books about how I got interested in photography, and how I began to seek out ways of producing images which were a bit 'different'— probably the result of taking too much interest in the work of Bill Brandt, Henri Cartier-Bresson, and various other major photographic figures in the Darlington Library. I have also described getting over some of the technical challenges facing people with high photographic ambition but not much cash. In particular, the art of cutting up 35-mm film in a sleeping bag, which must seem a mystery to those who have never tried it.

Let me explain: a standard thirty-six-exposure 35-mm film is about 6 feet long, but the small ads of the photographic press offered cans with 100-foot lengths of the same film at a fraction of the unit cost, provided you could transform one long length of film into around sixteen shorter ones, securely housed in cassettes. Everything had to be done in total darkness. If you had a dark room, it was a tedious but ultimately straightforward job to slice up the contents of the film can and emerge with cassettes ready for the camera. No dark room? Time to get the old but light-proof sleeping bag out, load it up with film, empty cassettes, scissors, and sticky tape, switch off the lights, and say to yourself several times, 'I will not lose my temper, come what may.'

Sometime later, maybe quite a lot later, you will have emptied the big film can, and loaded up several cassettes. In the meantime, it will become very hot, the sticky tape will have attached itself to many things you wanted it to leave alone, cassettes which opened and closed easily in daylight will have jammed, the scissors vanished, and general morale moved from apprehension to frustration and despair.

But on the bright side, loads of low-cost film and then plenty of time to walk around lead up to what now, after many decades, have become the illustrations in this book. With hindsight, I was lucky: I got better kit later in life, and tended to take fewer photographs with a lot more care. But the combination of a reasonable camera (after 1966, an Exakta Varex IIb, previously a couple of Zeiss products) and a lot of cheap film provided opportunities to be spontaneous and experimental in ways which just didn't happen when I was running full-price stock through a Hasselblad many years later. So maybe it was all for the best, but basically, who knows?

Getting around the place was not entirely straightforward either. During the 1960s, I was living in Darlington, which is about 16 miles from Stockton or Middlesbrough, 20 miles or so to the coast proper, the best part of 40 miles from Sunderland, and so on. Sometimes I had to be in these places for other reasons, like a job interview or during my brief career as a teenage van driver. It was not always possible to slip the bulky Exakta under my coat, but it went with me as often as I could manage it.

That aside, I had a bike (later a feeble motorbike, and after that occasional access to my mother's car). There were buses, and like many railway enthusiasts I was aware of travel opportunities which did not necessarily require the payment of a full fare. In the 1960s, hitchhiking was a reasonable option on some routes.

So one way or another I managed to get from place to place: I must have done, the photographic evidence is there. Mainly, I suspect, the big issue was being younger, fitter, and having more intellectual curiosity than I do now. If all else failed, there was walking, sometimes over considerable distances, and not always voluntarily. I remember pushing a motorbike for several miles when it ran out of fuel one night.

As traditional industries came under attack, people and communities suffered the consequences. For generations sons had followed their fathers down mines, onto the railways, or into steelworks, shipyards, and engineering works. But these options were melting away, and all too often 'change' really meant layoffs and closures.

I got talking to people when I was out and about taking photographs: they often seemed to be able to break off from what they were doing to have a chat, usually telling me, 'There's nothing around here worth taking a picture of.' If I asked, 'Can I take a picture of you?' it was rare to get any sort of refusal. Much more common were direct requests to 'tek mi picture, mista!' I recall a couple of people asking for prints, and that wasn't always possible—I struggled to get darkroom time, and it was sometimes years before everything was processed through to the final print. All I can say is that if you see yourself or a friend or a relative in these images, get in touch with me via the publishers and I'll get a print to you, with my apologies for the delay.

Looking back, I wish I'd taken a lot more photographs, but I suppose everybody says that. I also wish I'd taken better notes about the subject matter. I'd like to be able to provide more precision in some of the captions, but simply can't remember much about what they show.

I do appreciate that the images have a high proportion of the 'dark and gritty' for subject matter. Perhaps I should have taken more sunny suburb images for balance, but a lot of the industrial areas simply were fairly black and grimy, more interesting (to me at least), and—as history has amply proved—faced with extinction.

Above all, this is an area with a lot of different stories to tell. I've touched on the Venerable Bede and the monastic tradition already; not too far away to the south is Whitby, site of the seventh-century synod which made fundamental decisions about how the Christian Church would be ordered in the British Isles; and to the north is Lindisfarne, Holy Island. So the area has produced edilluminated manuscripts as well as riveted steelwork and pop music talent. Then there is a massive football tradition about which, as a Darlington supporter, I intend to say very little. And you can never ignore the sea: many generations have made their livings from it, whether as fishermen, makers and menders of ships, in the harbours and docks, or crewing vessels all over the world.

There is—or was—more to the coal industry than pitheads. As well as winding gear, the landscape featured washing and screening equipment, then conveyors and hoppers to get everything into railway wagons and away.

Pitmen (not usually 'miners' in Durham) walking home along the railway track past the Philadelphia workshops at the end of the shift; 'don't even think of getting a job doon the pit.'

And almost everywhere, shapes and angles, and people too. These were taken looking down from the Middlesbrough Transporter Bridge. For a photographer who gets books by Cartier-Bresson and Ansel Adams out of Darlington Library, there seemed to be a lot to get excited about.

Fishing: a perenially popular pastime. By fishing I mean repeatedly immersing line and bait in the waves; not necessarily extracting anything silvery from them.

Older men meet up to talk about all manner of things: politics, 'young people', 'how it used to be'. Maybe they're not technically past working age, but there are no jobs for people like them—or so they tell me. They don't see too many people with cameras. The most frequent question: 'Why would anyone want to take pictures round here?'Even if men were not in conventional employment, there were Things To Be Done: in sheds, on piers, in public parks, and all sorts of other places. What sort of Things? Well, it wouldn't be appropriate to say too much. You have to be a man of a certain age to understand.

I am determined to leave this section on a positive note. Even within an overall industrial picture which has tended to have more downs than ups since the Second World War, we must never forget that Nissan's plant at Washington now makes more cars per year than the whole of the Italian motor industry. And there are other success stories too, just not quite enough of them—so far. The final images for this section were taken at travelling fairs in the North East, another traditional antidote to hard work in heavy industries.

Nice beach; nice view of the steelworks as a backdrop, if you like that sort of thing.

It looks to be of great age and antiquarian interest and at 50 feet high, it's far from small. The truth is, it dates from 1844, and commemorates the life and works of the first Earl of Durham. It is said to have come in useful as a marker point for German bombers heading for the Tyneside factories and shipyards.

Above and below: A partial antidote to hard work in traditional industries: the fair comes to town.

Along the 'Sailor's Trod' paralleling the river and the railway on Teesside: 'Tek mi picture, mista!'

2

In and Around Teesside

The plan for the rest of this book is to work roughly south to north, which means making a start with Teesside and the surrounding areas.

Like a lot of other places in Britain, there wasn't a lot here until the Victorian era and a major catalyst for change was the Stockton and Darlington Railway. One end was, as you might expect, at Stockton. The other end wasn't at Darlington at all, for it was only about halfway to the real target, the coal mines around Bishop Auckland and Shildon. But those mines were capable of producing a great deal of coal and the access to deep(ish) water at Stockton was the key to getting a lot of it to market. Indeed, Stockton was maybe too successful for its own good, because the need for extra capacity led to the construction of docks at Middlesbrough and a much reduced role for Stockton.

But there was a lot more to come: Gladstone was soon to identify Middlesbrough as an 'infant Hercules' as furnaces and factories proliferated. Iron ore was available in the nearby Cleveland Hills: that helped the local iron works to grow, and in due course a major steel industry developed from the iron works. It made sense to set up foundries and fabrication sites to use local iron and steel products; soon access to deep water and a workforce used to shifts attracted the chemicals industry. And so it went on for quite a while, but not for ever.

So, thinking of Teesside in the 1960s inevitably brings to mind large-scale industries, not necessarily too fussed about what went up the chimney or down those pipes into the river.

But that wasn't quite fair. If you stayed on the trains from Darlington going beyond Middlesbrough, the first few miles were certainly spectacular for lovers of heavy industry. After that, though, it soon became rural and coastal, ending up in the delightful seaside town of Saltburn—another development triggered by the Stockton and Darlington Railway, but one with a distinctly genteel style not quite in the same category as Cargo Fleet and Dormanstown, just a few miles away to the north. Picturesque scenes came much sooner to passengers for Whitby or Guisborough, as the suburbs melted away into the fringes of the green Cleveland hills.

Timing is important when we think about Teesside. This book mainly focuses on the 1960s. Several organisations were certainly feeling the heat from remorseless and sophisticated competition from abroad, but investment was still going in elsewhere. British Steel was modernising its facilities; ICI had big plans; and oil in the North Sea was obviously going to be important, not just as a feedstock but maybe for fabrication work too.

Some of this investment really did happen. But by 1987, the Iron Lady was taking a walk across part of derelict Stockton. By this time guarded optimism about the fate of traditional industry really had been torn up and trampled on. In the 1960s, however, heavy industry still had a big story to tell, and it did so without much in the way of modesty or consideration for the neighbours.

I have shown these images to people from the home counties and other faraway places, some of whom say they find it all 'a bit dark, a bit grim'. I understand why they would say things like that, and fully subscribe to current efforts to talk the place up. But in Middlesbrough in the 1960s, there was still plenty of evidence of Gladstone's 'infant Hercules'. For me, a lot of its charm came through the muscular and unashamedly functional way of life this lusty little chap had adopted. From the top of the Transporter Bridge it did look as if he had put a grubby thumb print across several square miles of the landscape, bringing chimneys, great works and factories, and just a few spires and parks peeping through the haze.

We'll come back to the fate of those factories and the hopes for new markets and technical opportunities. It betrays few secrets to report that the story is not, overall, a particularly happy one. But back to the 1960s and the banks of the River Tees.

Heavy industry on Teesside: plenty of it in the 1960s, difficult to miss.

Left and below: Saltburn: relaxing, maybe a little bit refined. Floral displays, the cliff railway, Italian gardens and promenades, and afternoon tea at the Zetland Hotel before it became flats. The pier was longer than it is now, but had in the past been even longer. A combination of bad weather and poorly navigated ships sailing through it proved difficult for the ironwork to resist.

Right and below: I was particularly
fond of Saltburn's stylish station.
Maybe a lot of the design elements
were standard features, used by
the Stockton and Darlington or
the North Eastern Railway all over
the place. But they came together,
including a through platform
for the Zetland Hotel, to give an
overall effect which was all about
a charming day out at the seaside,
and had little or nothing to do with
iron, steel, chemicals, shipping, and
all that stuff just a handful of miles
away.

Above and left: Yarm, on the banks of the Tees. Upstream and on the way to beautiful dales countryside, but not so very far away from a lot of heavy industry in the 1960s.

At the start of the 1960s, a lot of industry still operated in ways you just don't see now. Road transport was improving all of the time, but computerised inventories and lean production were a long way off. All manner of products, spares, and sundries not only travelled in open, unbraked railway trucks: they were stored in them until needed, too. But railway tracks work in one dimension only—forwards and backwards—so spurs, sidings, and shunting yards were essential—lots of them.

The Teesside haze could give depth and perspective to some views, though it meant dullness and low contrast for many others. You might, at a pinch, draw parallels with Venice at sunset. But this was no passing effect from mists and sea breezes: it came from foundries, open fires, furnaces, coke ovens, and steam engines. I'm not exactly in favour of air pollution (nor water or land pollution, if it comes to that). But maybe we need to just spare a quick thought for views like this—you rarely see them these days. And have we simply exported the pollution? Certainly, Britain now relies on other nations for a lot of the things that we used to export all over the world from Teesside's mills and factories.

Maybe it's pretentious to talk about artistry in industrial brickwork, but you have to admire the work of those who could lay brick after brick with such precision.

Big strong shapes with complex shadows: somehow or other, this impressive stand of reeds has survived through all the so-called environmental damage to stand out nicely in the low afternoon sun. Surprisingly appealing (well, I thought so). Interestingly, reed beds are a major success story—widely used these days because of their roots' ability to absorb some of the world's nastier pollutants.

Above and right: The Sailors'
Trod, paralleling the railway and
the river, was a footpath extending
over several miles with unrivalled
views of steelworks and other
visual attractions—for a certain
kind of visitor only.

There even seemed to be opportunities for expansion and new directions. With oil starting to be pumped from under the North Sea, all manner of platforms and rigs were needed: why not build them in an area with a great tradition of making all sorts of big things out of metal? Somehow or other, these hopes never quite got fulfilled.

You can still walk over the top of the Transporter Bridge if minded to do so, though one factor to bear in mind is the little matter of the £4 ticket, rather than the 'coppers-if-you're-daft-enough' approach I remember from the 1960s.

Climbing over the bridge superstructure isn't for everyone. You have to be fairly fit and reasonably determined to climb all the stairs, and it isn't much good for those nervous about heights, obviously. I'm not nervous about heights, and have never questioned the safety built into each part of this wonderful structure, but at the top of it all there can be little doubt that you are quite a way up in the fresh air, with a long drop to the sullen river and grimy wharves.

One of the few constant features in the landscape has been the Transporter Bridge, and I took a lot of photographs of it during the 1960s and subsequently. Its function then was a bit different: a genuine solution to transport needs, across a river where shipping still mattered.

Like most estuaries, the lower stretches of the Tees were very different at high tide and low tide. The high tide concealed a lot of sins and, photographically speaking, gave opportunities for capturing reflections and a certain amount of peaceful stillness.

Like a lot of other ports, houses had been built close to where the ships berthed in Middlesbrough, with all the usual arguments about community and convenience on the one hand and worries about poor quality, potential disturbance from noise, and dust on the other. Anyway, down they came.

It was not just the docks; similar houses in similar streets elsewhere got the same treatment.

My first proper job was on Teesside. It was in ICI's Wilton Works, on the south bank and hence in Yorkshire. I might well have ended up at Billingham, firmly in County Durham. I shall always be grateful to Wilton for helping me make an important career choice: although I had a university place to read sciences, I had no real idea of what that might mean in practice. At Wilton I began to see some of my limitations: it wasn't that I was hopeless at science, it was just that plenty of people were obviously better scientists than I was likely to become, and I never regretted switching to economics. I was probably competent (or close) at lab work, but sometimes the necessary precision eluded me. Thinking up three points for an essay and knocking out some conclusions? That was more like it.

No one should doubt my commitment to ICI Wilton. The trip there each morning required a certain amount of effort and went as follows: get up in Darlington and walk to the station; day return ticket to South Bank on the (then fairly new) diesel multiple unit; walk through South Bank to the main road; then a Teesside Railless Traction Company bus to the factory gate; and finally an internal bus to the lab. And the whole lot had to be carried out in reverse each evening.

I wouldn't say the work was interesting, but it was varied. I didn't realise it, but there was an initiation test. One task for those working in my lab involved climbing steel lattice stairs to the top of the vent pipes above a series of massive storage tanks and taking samples of the gases. With no personal fear of heights I got on and did it, not exactly rushing and taking time to admire the sun on the Cleveland hills just a few miles away to the south. It turned out that most of my new colleagues didn't like this job at all, and hoped to see a repeat of previous cases of pallor, shaking, or occasional vomiting.

I learned a lot at Wilton. In the works canteen I had my first encounter with the spam fritter. Out on the plant I soon met the great British industrial tradition of blaming someone else if there were problems. In this case, we produced intermediaries to be worked on by others, and most of the critical feedback came from a plant in Wales. I soon noted key phrases like, 'It was all right when it left here,' and 'Don't blame me if those Welsh boys don't know what they're doing.'

This page and opposite: The Tees Transporter Bridge: it dominated the local landscape, and still performed a useful transportation function. Certainly, it was a long way round on the rare occasions when it was out of service. Photographically speaking, the Transporter Bridge offered so many opportunities: close-up, the generous details of its original construction were plain to see; and local people took a lot of pride in it. Sometimes this pride went a bit too far, with talk of the Tees Transporter Bridge being 'unique' or 'the last in the world'. It's a wonderful piece of engineering, but it's not the only one; something very similar crosses the River Usk at Newport, for example.

The paddle tug *John H. Amos*: subsequently preserved and—despite a somewhat difficult few years—with us still.

Above and opposite: Moored in the lower reaches of the Tees were various vessels of varying sizes and shapes. Some looked grimy but seaworthy. Others were on an unhurried conversion from 'floating but not worth mending' to definite wrecks, rusting away on the bank in pieces. Picturesque? Well, certainly, with a bit of imagination.

This page and opposite: Ships and things that go on ships in various states of decay. High tide on the Tees; reflections and, particularly in the evenings, an aura of stillness and peace, despite the heavy industry all around, and a long history of busy commercial activity. Though much straightened and dredged, this was, after all, the waterway that attracted the promoters of the Stockton and Darlington Railway, seeking to get all that profitable coal to waiting markets.

Low tide was rather different, and revealed large quantities of glossy, chocolate-coloured mud. On the mud—or rather, partly engulfed by it—was nautical debris of many varieties. The barren ribs of long-gone barges and coasters, inverted hulls unlikely to float again, anchors, cables, chains ... all manner of things to do with boats. Wonderful material for photographs. Not everybody saw it in these terms, however, and I suppose that if you tried to find suitable words to describe the mud itself, 'fresh' and 'fragrant' would not be among them.

Above: A quick visit to Middlesbrough docks. The single ship in the background seems to be one of the Ellerman's 'City Line' vessels (possibly *City of Port Elizabeth*), nice-looking ships from an age where the British merchant marine could be found almost anywhere in the world, shifting goods and passengers for just about anyone who could pay. But these were not big vessels (around 10,000 tons' displacement) and had substantial crews (often well over 100), which left them hopelessly vulnerable to containerisation and mass air travel. The diesel shunter in the foreground is, well, a diesel shunter. You can yearn for a (steam) J72 or even a J94 for as long as you like: they've been sent on the one-way trip to North Road scrapyard.

Above left, right and opposite below: More views of the docks: when opened in the first half of the nineteenth century, so new and modern, they completely eclipsed the facilities on the Durham side of the river, at Stockton. By now cluttered, congested, and really too small for the way things were going in world shipping, they were subsequently redeveloped to provide sites for enterprises like the new football stadium. Whether this would be a massive surprise to people working in the docks at the time I can't easily tell. It was obvious enough that the number of ships using the port had declined substantially; despite a good deal of militant industrial action from dockers—particularly in London and Liverpool—traditional ways of working were being rolled back, year by year, by containerisation and general growth in ship sizes and mechanisation. There was to be no easy transition; organised labour took part in bitter struggles with British ship-owners and port employers. But behind it all lay even more powerful international commercial interests and inexorable technical change.

Left, below and opposite: Houses near the docks: objectively, not great houses perhaps. But handy for work for a lot of people, and neighbours who looked out for each other. They had survived the attentions of the Luftwaffe; they didn't do so well against the wrecking ball.

With the shipping business well down and local communities being slum-cleared away, the pub trade inevitably suffered.

Similar factors hit other traditional pastimes, like playing naturally and confidently in the street.

Above and below: This is supposed to be a book about everyday life, and these views of Middlesbrough show little else. So everyday is the subject matter that I'm not even sure why I took them: it's possible I was just finishing a film off, but now I'm glad I pressed the shutter. With the passage of time all sorts of details they contain have simply vanished.

Left, below and next four pages: Industry on Teesside. I worked in a chemical plant which was 3 miles long by 2 miles wide; the train ride to get there went through the heart of the steel industry. Lovers of England's green and pleasant land may demur, but if you like the Tate Modern, surely you must get mildly excited about facilities which were on an even bigger scale. These didn't rely on carefully crafted artworks to create an effect, but generated great clouds of steam and fumes of their own. After dark the steel plants came into their own with cauldrons of red hot slag and rivers of molten metal lighting up the towering black shapes around them. I had a go at taking some impressionistic night-time photos, but the necessary techniques eluded me.

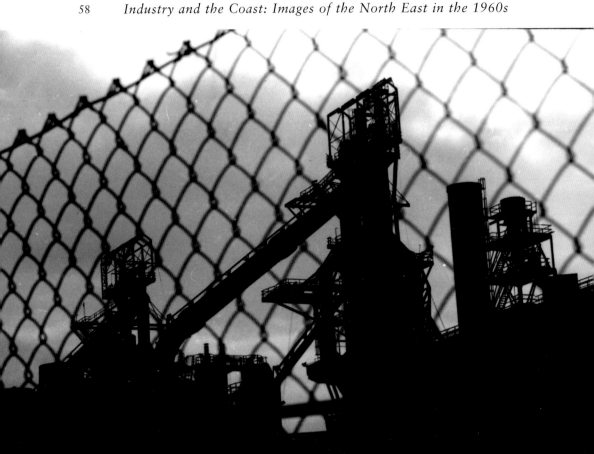

Diesel multiple units at Darlington Station: part of the fleet that carried me to South Bank every day for a while.

Many years later I happened to do some consultancy work in the self-same Welsh factory, where several people told me, 'We've no chance of hitting targets unless Wilton stop sending rubbish!'

Whatever some of the customers might say, it seemed to me that I was working in a modern, well managed operation, even if sometimes accidents did happen. I think they do in most manufacturing environments. When something went wrong, it usually involved substances venting skywards. Then top scientists would make crucial risk assessments—not so much for the benefit of surrounding communities, but concerning the paintwork of their own cars and those of their friends. If necessary an informal system swung into place, far slicker than anything operated by management, in which car owners moved their vehicles to an appropriate place of safety, carefully attuned to the likely consequences when what had just taken to the air came back down to earth.

Above and below: Not too far from all that heavy industry, the cool waters of the North Sea and the beaches at Redcar.

Above, left and opposite: Small business wasn't entirely crowded out. It was soon apparent that all those laboursaving gadgets which rising prosperity in the 1960s brought within reach didn't solve every problem, not by any means, and they were far from maintenance-free themselves. Houses needed painting, motorcars mending—and there was so much else. These are the best examples I have from the area, although from Whitby rather than Teesside itself.

Above and below: To keep a bit of balance with a reminder of the rural areas all around, I've included further images of the group of superannuated railway coaches providing shelter on a farm in North Yorkshire. My eye was caught particularly by the elegant details on each end panel.

Above, right and next page: Yet we all know where this is heading. As time went by, a lot of noisy, black, heavy engineering sites became silent, green public open space, through processes which past generations of workers just wouldn't have understood. Indeed, it wasn't easy for a lot of people to think of newly landscaped, environmentally approved areas as an unalloyed improvement on what had come before. Hard-won fabrication skills were used to make steel dinosaurs. Honestly, they were. Think of the little matter of all those thousands of jobs and hurt pride over Britain's lost status in world manufacturing.

This did not happen very often, but regular minor leaks and venting tended to make the phrases 'downwind' and 'fresh air' mutually incompatible. Years later, when I came across the health statistics for nearby communities like Dormanstown and Cargo Fleet, they weren't a total surprise.

Anyhow, with vital lessons learned, a few months later I more than doubled my pay and halved my travel time to work by taking on a job at the civil engineering site which was to become the A1 (M). More of that later.

3

Coast and Countryside

There's enough variety on the Durham coast to cover most purposes and interests. However, we do again stray further afield, as far as Whitby in a couple of cases. Attractive though a lot of the North Yorkshire coast is now (and was fifty years ago), the distinction with Durham isn't as sharp as all that: North Yorkshire has coastal industries (like the Skinningrove iron and steel works) which would fit into the industrial parts of County Durham well enough. Yet the Durham coast is far from being all mills and mines. It really does (and did) have several miles of white or golden sand, in many cases quite close to the sites of traditional heavy industries.

So it was a mixed picture in the 1960s. There was plenty of evidence of serious industrial activity along the coast, but that wasn't the whole story. Where tipping was controlled and litter was collected reasonably often, there could be sandy beaches of a quality you just wouldn't get in a lot of so-called resorts. And The Denes—deep, wooded valleys stretching almost to the shoreline—were (and still are) distinctive and attractive, often providing a refuge for all manner of animal and plant life.

It's just that other stretches weren't doing that sort of job at all, and maybe through some perverse inverted beauty contest had been nominated to collect the unwanted detritus of all sorts of human activity: coal, brick, sewage—you name it. Dotted along the coast itself were not just massive collieries but chemical works, breweries, and other neighbours with solid, liquid, and gaseous materials they simply wanted to get rid of as quickly and cost-effectively as possible.

Away from the coast it was mainly farming, but again graced by coal mines and various other developments, most of which could be relied on to make a contribution to the less satisfactory aspects of local environmental standards.

Much of this has changed over the past half-century, of course, with the Durham coast starting to fit seamlessly into the gap between the rugged beauties of the North Yorkshire coast and the sweeping sands, castles, and intriguing islands which fringe Northumberland. The missing ingredient? Basically coal: as the pits have closed, and tipping waste into the sea has ceased, the beaches have improved a lot.

Above and opposite: Dramatic coastal features.

Above and below: And coalmining….

Yet for a long time coastal pits represented hope and prosperity. Coal seams in the North East tend to thicken and deepen from West to East. Coal had been mined near the coast for many years, but some of the most productive seams were overlain by hazardous sands or the infamous magnesian limestone, both prone to send water into a newly excavated shaft faster than any pumps could remove it. Eventually, more reliable shaft-sinking technologies were developed, including freezing the wet ground then excavating and lining shafts quickly before the water could reappear.

Before long it was time to dig coal and move some serious tonnage. And in the 1960s, those fat, rich seams trailing away under the North Sea looked as if they would meet customer needs, and keep miners working for a long time to come.

That's not the way it worked out, of course, and the Durham coal industry, which at one time had 304 pits employing 165,000 people had, by the end of 1993 lost its final deep mine, Wearmouth (Lynemouth in Northumberland lasted a year longer).

Some of these trends might well have been apparent in a general sort of way in the 1960s, but I think it's safe to say that the total loss of the coal mining industry within a couple of decades wasn't envisaged by anyone. The loss of coal mining set events in motion well away from the pitheads. Ports and harbours which once relied on shifting a single, black commodity had to find new roles—replacing coal chutes with marinas, no less. Tipping waste into the sea has stopped, improving the quality of beaches and seawater no end, but reducing the scope for men with sacks and old bikes to scrape up the 'sea coal'.

Lots of changes in the North East in the 1960s were part of trends which covered much longer time spans and much wider areas. The decline of North East shipbuilding is an example of long-term shifts in global markets over most of the post-war period. So it has been with 'green' issues and improving the environment; local action has to be seen in a context of international campaigning, lobbying, treaties, and the rest. Voters became interested in these issues, and it wasn't long before what had been overlooked or tolerated for generations became unacceptable.

In and around County Durham, there has been much tidying up, assuaging some of the guilt from past irreverence to Mother Nature perhaps. Some have argued that pollution has partly been exported, not obliterated. Closing a factory in Stockton while opening a similar one in China might just have this effect. In any case, the area has undeniably seen pollution levels fall; as a general rule, however, it has missed the Holy Grail of building greener, sustainable communities with high levels of employment in new industries, to replace all those traditional jobs and hence reinvigorate 'run-down' local areas. Hopes of attracting new, science-based industries have generally been dashed.

Back to images of life in the 1960s. It's convenient to start by moving north from Teesside along the coast. The first few miles have nothing to do with the coal trade, and aren't much like anywhere else in the area. These estuarial flatlands have seen a good deal of development in recent years, but in the decade in question had more mud than sand, and human habitation down around the levels only seen in the high moorlands, way to the west.

Very little in the way of recreational sailing, by today's standards. This example is at Whitby.

Above and opposite above: Even in the 1960s, some excellent beaches, and far from crowded. The local authorities also made some attempts to attract visitors, although 'chilly' was as good a word as any to describe the bathing experience in the North Sea.

The simplest thing to say about what went direct into the sea is to record that practices and attitudes were about to change. But in the 1960s colliery waste in vast quantities was still tipped straight into the North Sea (remember the original *Get Carter?*). Plenty of other stuff went the same way. And here the sunlight twinkles nicely in the effluent, racing into the welcoming North Sea.

Heading north from Teesside. Big skies, (relatively) fresh air—and a lot of mud.

Looking back to Teesside, all that industry was still very much there: a brutal fist hammering at the skyline but for a few miles between Billingham and Hartlepool, the view was dominated by grass and mud, and sea and sky.

There are nature reserves as well as prefabricated industrial units now, but in the 1960s matters were less controlled and the main things I recall about the trip from Billingham, say, to West Hartlepool were of all of that mud, a flat landscape with a big sky and the very strange sights at Greetham Creek.

Amid complicated little inlets and blocks of salt marsh, old boats had been lifted out of the water, then all manner of additions made—often in driftwood, sometimes in smartly varnished prime timber. They ended up as what I suppose would be the fisherman's equivalent of a shed on the allotment, maybe even a second home. And it wasn't just one or two—there were dozens of them.

I have subsequently read a bit more about this colourful community of old boats and the people who used them, but at the time knew none of this. The images here are really those of a tourist: I saw something which looked interesting from the Hartlepool train and on a couple of occasions later on got off at Greatham Station, next to the Cerebos salt factory, and got walking.

The houseboats were just as picturesque as I had hoped, with fascinating details; careful reuse of all kinds of material; and systematic conservation of rainwater. But I never saw a soul there to put life into the place, and didn't even manage to catch a high tide when I bet everything looked a whole lot better, with something to reflect all that sky. Ah well.

Hartlepool isn't far away. Before we get there, just a brief excursion to stress that, despite all the industry, Mother Nature had not been obliterated. Wildflowers

Teesside from the north: the steam clouds from another load of quenched coke try to compete with nature's cumulonimbus, late on a winter afternoon.

Man-made structures were typically functional, rather than elegant (here at Seaham Harbour).

Above, below and opposite: Houseboats at Greetham Creek: neat, orderly, close to nature, with high levels of sustainability—and all without the benefit of advice from the town planning fraternity. Presumably agents would think in terms of 'unique features to match the lifestyle of each lucky owner' or 'customised detailing within the same eco-friendly design parameters.' Or is that just being gratuitously unkind to skilled professionals?

Some of the contrasts: flowers flourished along the clifftops (in this case near Seaham).

Above left and right: The Denes: home of the Durham Argus: no, not a newspaper, and not entirely unique to the area, as I found out later.

flourished on the clifftops, and, while fly-tipping was not unknown, there was plenty of wildlife in the Denes, as they cut down to the sea. Many years ago, I was told on what I thought was good authority that the Castle Eden Dene was home for a unique butterfly, the Durham Argus. It's a good job I checked. Despite its unique name, which you might think ought to be on an evening newspaper, it turns out that this is merely a sub-species of the Northern Argus, which you can—apparently—find in plenty of places, if you know what to look for. Now I wouldn't recognise a Durham Argus if one landed on the keyboard in front of me, but I would have relished writing about something rare and attractive on this coastline, the backdrop of so many activities which couldn't be classed as either rare or attractive.

And so to Hartlepool. It's a reasonable question to ask why I have included so few images of Hartlepool, and so many of, say, Seaham. I've nothing against Hartlepool: I've spent many hours there, I've watched football and rugby (and played rugby) there. I don't really care whether they hung the monkey or not, and admire them for spotting Brian Clough's managerial skills first.

I actually did take several hundred photographs around Hartlepool in the 1960s, but here's the rub: up to about the middle of 1967, if you were a railway enthusiast and wanted to take photographs of steam engines, you had to do little more than stand by the side of the coast line at West Hartlepool. A procession of steam-powered freight came past—mostly coal, but also shifting steel billets and sections, limestone, and all the other commodities heavy industry either swallows or spits out. And for every loaded train going one way, there was usually an empty one coming back, along with various light engine movements, and fussing around with brake vans and short strings of transfers. There was so much to watch, other attractions never got much attention.

At Seaham, however, a trip to take photographs of asthmatic tank engines shuffling around the mighty coal staithes could end up delivering no such images if there wasn't any work to do, or a lorry or steam crane could do it. So having a look at anything and everything else was only natural.

When planning this book I thought I wouldn't aim to include anything unduly serious, but when thinking of Seaham in the 1960s, a serious tone is inescapable. Late one November afternoon in 1962, a lifeboat was launched with a crew of five local men to go to the assistance of a local fishing boat caught out in a sudden, vicious, and worsening storm. With considerable skill in appalling conditions, the fishing boat's crew of four men and a nine-year-old boy were rescued, but when trying to re-enter the harbour the lifeboat was capsized by mountainous seas. There was only one survivor, and he was one of the fishermen.

This area is no stranger to tragedy: accidents in the mines killed hundreds over the years. But I defy anyone not to be deeply moved by some of the evidence given at the inquest into the loss of life when the lifeboat capsized, for all of this happened within yards of the harbour entrance, with locals on the shore desperate to find any means of averting the disaster unfolding in front of them. Men were

Above and below: The coastal geology has always been worth looking at, if you could ignore the 'sea coal' and the like. The sea carves various stacks and arches out of the limestone for a while then cuts them down too. Photographically, a lot depends on the time of day: what's grey and dull and solid in sunlight can be brooding, mysterious, and almost menacing in the twilight.

What the fuss was all about: steam power, in this case a Q6 0-8-0 hauling coal along the busy railway line skirting the North Sea. Part of a parade of wonderful steam engines to admire, mostly designed by the North Eastern Railway Company half a century earlier.

A scene that typifies a lot of train travel in this area in the 1960s: waiting for the stopping train to turn up at West Hartlepool, while yet another string of coal hoppers trundle by.

Above and below: Token gestures: a couple of Hartlepool's street scenes. Most of the time, though, I was focusing on the railway lines.

Above and below: In those days, West Hartlepool had a reasonable beach, but local people didn't seem to take much interest in it. Hence the untidy piles of concrete castings—part of a programme which would at least shift effluent discharge a bit further away from the shore. The concrete path at the top of the beach was no Mediterranean Corniche: more, well, a concrete path at the top of the beach.

General view of Seaham: coal exporting to the south (right), fishing to the north (left).

Interested observer: lifeboat station behind.

able to cling to the upturned hull of the lifeboat for a while: it was so close to the shore the only survivor described feeling the upturned mast dragging in the shingle on the beach. But such was the power of the storm that nine lives were lost, and the story became shocking news across the globe.

I didn't go to Seaham until later in the decade; I knew well enough what had happened, but tragedy was so difficult to envisage. Most of the time everything was, well, so quiet. I saw one smallish storm and there was something malevolent and chilling about the waves breaking over the harbour wall, but this clearly wasn't in the same league as the seas the brave lifeboat men had faced.

Now Seaham Harbour really has seen vast change since the 1960s. No sign of any marina then, of course: this was very much a working environment, but with two distinct elements.

To the north, the harbour retained the traditional emphasis on fishing: predominantly small, inshore boats following traditional designs to be able to work among the rocks and waves which can be so hazardous, even for the lifeboat.

Nets had to be dried, crab pots mended, broken bits of kit disposed of. Maybe it looked disorganised and untidy to some; to others there was at least the same appeal offered by Whitby or the Cornish fishing ports. I was, and remain, firmly in the second group.

The docks to the south were profoundly different in almost every way. Developed in stages by the Londonderry family and their successors, this was a facility with one function only: getting the ample coal from local pits into specialist collier vessels quickly, cheaply, and in substantial quantity.

The technology for the transfer at the staithes could hardly have been simpler: strings of loaded railway wagons were manoeuvred along high-level wooden or concrete staithes until aligned with the top end of particular iron chutes. When the doors were released or wagon rotated, a load of Durham's finest thundered down the chutes into the appropriate ship's hold below. More of the same would follow, then it was time for some trimming and levelling, and off on the next tide.

Now that doesn't quite do justice to the scale of things. From the side of the dock, the staithes had the same sort of dimensions as the pillars in Durham Cathedral, and something of their solemnity and grandeur too. You got a better feeling of how big everything was when the staithes were demolished, but that was much later, towards the end of the 1970s.

There were normally various people around the place. The whole complex needed operating and maintaining, so there were usually men with flat hats and shovels around somewhere or other. More generally there were no barriers to simply wandering around the dock and harbour at Seaham. I took advantage of this enlightened policy on several occasions and there were usually other people doing much the same. It was, well, an interesting sort of place. The men charged with maintenance and other duties would often have a chat too. So if you needed a human figure to improve the composition of a particular photograph, you didn't have to wait long for somebody to turn up.

A storm at Seaham. Puny by comparison with the evening when the lifeboat was lost, but I wouldn't want to have been anywhere near that wave slamming over the harbour wall.

Next three pages: Fishermen, fishing boats, and fishing paraphernalia in part of the Seaham Harbour complex.

Above and opposite: The staithes at Seaham had the capacity to shift a lot of coal quickly. I never saw them at their busiest, and much more typical were sights like these, with one or two vessels filling their holds only. The ship tied up facing the camera has the low bridge and retractable masts needed to get under the Thames bridges, ready to supply customers like Battersea Power Station.

Above and next three pages: Seen from the dockside, the staithes were very impressive indeed—
sometimes compared to standing in a forest of very tall trees, or the nave of a cathedral. In truth,
they were bigger than that. And among it all, evidence of what merchant seamen thought of it
during their brief stay for loading.

Below: Simple but effective machinery for transferring coal from train to ship with the minimum fuss.

Above, below and opposite: A busy port needs plenty of tugs, and these included one of the very last paddle tugs in operation, *Reliant. Reliant* even made it to preservation at the National Maritime Museum, but that didn't guarantee survival. Controversially, she was still scrapped some years later. Too big? Possibly, but it was never really clear why *Reliant* was deemed 'the wrong kind of heritage'.

Demolition came in the 1970s. Look at the scale of the chutes by comparison with those tiny human figures; think of how much coal had raced down them.

Above, below and next two pages: People in an industrial landscape at Seaham.

And now a word about wagons. In the normal course of things, I'd probably say that anyone taking any level of detailed interest in railway wagons should be seeking help. But dotted around the side of the dock at Seaham were objects with a direct link to the very earliest days of coal mining and railway development in the North East. These chaldron wagons were a bit bigger than those you can see in etchings of the opening of the Stockton and Darlington Railway in 1825, but the basic design is the same, and indeed goes back to well before the S&DR. For the imaginative, the hulks at Seaham had a kind of faded grandeur because of this extraordinary pedigree. If that was too fanciful, you could at least admire wonderful textures and colours in wood and wrought iron which had been subjected to all sorts of use and misuse.

This part of the coast had pits, and hence pit villages deemed to have a definite future, with a couple of exceptions. Indeed, one justification for running down villages elsewhere (we consider the 'Category D' policy in the book on the West of this area) was that miners would be able to secure long-term jobs if they moved east to places like these. And there were good jobs for a while, but the strikes in the 1980s were bitter, and not long afterwards deep mining was gone from the county altogether.

Before leaving this part of the coast, a quick word about sea coal and sea coaling. For many years, the beaches along this coast were prone to deliver strands of coal particles, eagerly harvested by men with sacks, to be removed from the beach across old bicycles, or sometimes on the back of one of the more careworn sorts of lorry. It may well be that some coal outcrops under the North Sea were naturally eroded by the waves and sent onto the shore. But it always did seem that the practice of tipping colliery waste direct into the waves played more than a part in it. It may be difficult to believe how much of this went on in our more environmentally queasy times, but those who remember *Get Carter*—the original Michael Caine version, not the remake—will have seen the evidence.

The men scraping up the sea coal had attracted the attention of various documentary photographers and there were tales of significant resentment at the treatment they had received (allegedly compounded by the interest shown by benefits officers in this harmless trade). I had no wish to infringe on people's privacy as they went about their business—this wasn't my kind of photography anyway—but here are just a couple of images of men, sacks, and bicycles.

I'm conscious I haven't said much about the areas inland. Do I think Sedgefield isn't worthy of attention? Not at all. What about the high hopes embodied in the Peterlee and Washington New Towns? I seem to have had a mental block about all New Towns. And what about that hotel and those very grand houses at Wynyard? That's easier—they hadn't yet been built.

I travelled through the countryside extensively. Cycling wasn't a great option going east from Darlo: the roads tended to be a lot busier than those going up the dales to the west. So maybe the affinity which comes from grinding slowly across a landscape didn't build up. Whatever—I just didn't take many photos. I have a few with steam engines at collieries, but that doesn't really capture much about the locality.

One part of inland Durham I came to know intimately was the site of the A1 (M), where I worked in a variety of jobs for several months in the summer of 1966. At the heart of my job was just keeping tabs on kit. Several pumps and (probably) a small dumper had been buried and lost on site because nobody knew they had gone missing. Then some contractors were a bit prone to forget to tell the company when their equipment had broken down and couldn't work, or, it was rumoured, when they were busily engaged at alternative tasks like tarmacking a local farmer's drive.

I had my own office: a redundant BR 10-ton container, which was fine because it meant I didn't need to go near the cabin where some of the hourly-paid men hung about. I have a strong stomach, but even the thought of the atmosphere in there—pungent with cheap tobacco, stale sweat, diesel, and last month's burnt bacon fat—could make me retch well into the 1980s.

I had spare time most days and was on a rota to run the switchboard for an hour a day to give the usual operator a break. I've had various jobs since, including a couple behind panelled doors which people knocked on before entering, but working this temporary switchboard in the middle of nowhere was certainly among the toughest. When all was going smoothly, no problem: good service, strong customer care, smiling faces all around. But when one thing went wrong it told its friends, and soon nobody was speaking to anybody over the phone, though a lot of yelling came echoing down the corridor.

Spells as a stand-in, unofficial earth-scraper driver were a lot more fun. These things aren't toys—at least I think that was what one of the foremen was shouting as a TS24 went over his foot on a wet afternoon (driven by a professional driver, not a happy amateur). Not that the 8-foot Michelins were really hard tyres: another pro told me so after clipping a dozer blade, ensuring instant deflation. He was on his way to his car and a career change after brief discussions with management at the time.

Also driven by a pro was one that rolled over as a result of too much dirt being held too high in a machine turning more quickly than it should on an adverse slope. Basically bad driving, most people said. But there was the mighty TS24, on its back like a tortured yellow beetle—a very big beetle nonetheless, with two large diesels screaming and four vast wheels still churning. I'm not sure if there was an automatic cut-off or one of the other drivers reached in to switch it off. Either way, a foremen showed real decency by checking the driver over carefully and making sure he was OK—before, that is, inviting him to pursue his career goals somewhere else.

Now back to the coast. After a good deal of talk about serious matters like industrial decline and housing demolition, it will seem odd to be ending this chapter on the much happier, almost frivolous theme of holidays and days out. But it's no joke: even in the era of tipping colliery waste straight into the sea, there were fine beaches. How many people made it the object of their summer holidays I don't know, but day-trippers were another matter and even stretches of sand quite close to the big coastal collieries could get busy.

I've included images from around Seaham, as well as the Sunderland to South Shields coastline, and, as usual, do need to apologise to communities like Seaton

Above and left: Chaldron wagons. Still in use for maintenance at Seaham in the 1960s, though soon to go to Beamish Museum because of their genuine historic value.

Above, below and next two pages: 'Modern' pits and pit villages. Prone to turn their backs on the bracing North Sea, but after all, these were not holiday resorts: the beaches would have been golden once, but not with mine waste being tipped straight into the waves.

Above and opposite: Seacoaling: men with second-hand sacks and third-hand bikes.

Above and below: Parts of the once-extensive network of private lines operated by the NCB in the North East. Equipped to operate in good and unfavourable weather.

Earth scraper driven by pro; A1 (M).

The finished product. Nearly ready to open the motorway.

Above, below and opposite: Eat your heart out, Brighton: the Durham coast has golden sands, not shingle. Councils contributed concrete structures, and other municipal features. The walkways and tasteful balustrading were prone to be overcome by drifting sand. I didn't deliberately picture the roof lights in the shelter to look as if a large, malevolent frog had been petrified below—but on the other hand, it was difficult to avoid showing something that looked distinctly threatening.

Above, below and opposite: From the private sector: amusements, ices, chips, and Frankie's Ritz ('Restaurant, Amusements, Kiddies' Rides').

Above, left and opposite: It could all add up to good numbers of visitors on a summer afternoon. Even in winter the hardier individuals came in ones and twos, well wrapped up against the cold winds from the east. And the waves called strongly to those who thought 60 degrees Fahrenheit merely 'bracing'.

Opposite, above and below: Visitors: a varied, hardy bunch....

Though stylish to admirers of modern trends in pit-head gear, mines near the golden beaches, and the knowledge that pitmen were toiling away at coalfaces several miles away under the sea, this probably didn't help marketing efforts.

Carew: unfortunately, despite visiting from time to time, I just don't have any images to show for it.

At these aspiring resorts, local councils contributed investments in promenades, unusual concrete castings, and planting schemes, while the private sector was ready with amusements, ices, and chips. To be fair that wasn't the whole story, what with a couple of mines working very close to the beach to give a backdrop not seen in Benidorm. And while I've been swimming in the North Sea many times, 'fresh' is a better way of describing the experience than 'warm'.

We've nearly reached the mouth of the Tyne and the end of this chapter. We'll finish off with a handful of pictures of visitors. Very varied, I think you'll agree.

4
Tyne and Wear

I have said on several occasions that this book isn't bound by precise boundaries: there are gaps and overlaps at several points. Even so, it must be obvious enough that I haven't said very much about the heavily populated and once heavily-industrialised areas in the north of Durham and south of Northumberland. Their turn comes now, although I am well aware of local sensitivities which can arise if we group them together, particularly in football-related matters. But can't we set this kind of animosity to one side for a while? The urban areas on the banks of the Tyne and Wear all came under the rule of the Tyne & Wear County Council for a time, after the 1972 Local Government Act was passed. The two rivers are only 7 miles apart at their mouths, and both have traditionally been heavily involved in shipbuilding and ancillary industries, and shipped coal in great quantities for many years. The other factor I have had to bear in mind is, to be honest, that I don't really have enough photographs of either to make good, solid separate chapters.

Let's start with some basics. It is true to say that the 1960s saw serious decline in several traditional industries in this part of the North East, but the processes took much more than a single decade to work through. There was no specific crisis point in the 1960s when a satisfactory outlook was transformed into an economic disaster. In the case of shipbuilding, Britain's long-established world leading-position for constructing merchant vessels started to erode not long after the Second World War, but the UK still had around 20 per cent of the world market at the start of the 1960s. Although this was down to about 6 per cent by 1969, further decline was a long drawn-out affair, with the UK retaining about 3 per cent of the world market as late as 1980.

There was no tame surrender either, but in a flurry of speeches, well-meaning reports, hasty defensive mergers, questionable management decisions and vicious industrial relations, first export markets were lost—35 per cent of the world export market for 1948–50 became 4.5 per cent in 1961–65—then the home market went the same way—100 per cent of deliveries to the UK-registered fleet in 1948–50 became 26 per cent by 1961–65.[1]

Similarly for the coal industry, decline was an undeniable reality during the 1960s. But we have to remember that several collieries lasted much longer than

Above and below: If you liked photographing shipyard cranes and Victorian terraced housing, this was no bad place to be. It has to be said that, by the 1960s, both were past their prime.

that, for example Murton (between Sunderland and South Shields , closed in 1991) and Westoe (South Shields, closed in 1993).[2]

So taking pictures of economic or urban decline as a backdrop to everyday life wasn't difficult, but there was more to it than that. The vast majority of people of working age were in work and, as we noted earlier, during the 1960s people, on average, became somewhat better off, leading to steady increases in sales of motorcars, domestic appliances, *etc.*

Let's start with Sunderland. The Tyneside metro wasn't built in the 1960s, nor the A19 much upgraded, so nobody got to Sunderland in a hurry. But the trips to Sunderland which really stand out in my memory were of a different sort altogether. They were unofficial trips on the footplate of steam engines.

I have already mentioned my fondness for the NCB's tank engines stabled at Philadelphia, and one of the duties for larger, more important locomotives was taking loaded coal trains from the pits around Houghton-le-Spring to Sunderland for shipping. A polite enquiry and you could be on the footplate, admiring the driver and fireman coaxing surprisingly lively performances from railway engines often fifty years old or more.

It seems fair to say that most footplatemen didn't quite 'get it' when it came to enthusiasts. Thoughtful, considerate people, they were prone to suggest travelling in the guard's van as a better means of keeping warm and dry than the cab. And, when all was said and done, what was so special about shining levers, a blazing grate, and a chime-whistle if that was what you worked with every day for many years? But they kindly indulged us, even though fitting in the driver, fireman, and a couple of enthusiasts called for a bit of care if the fireman was going to swing his shovel as well.

There were two destinations in Sunderland: the South Dock, which was relatively modern, and the Sunderland Staithes, which weren't. These were the former Lambton Staithes, or Lambton Drops, on a constricted site down by the river and close to the centre of Sunderland. The site had been rebuilt and revised many times, but the basic model of shifting coal to ships berthed in the Wear using wagons running on steel, iron, or wooden rails goes back to the early part of the eighteenth century, amazingly.

To get to the staithes meant passing through Doxford's shipyards, past a sinister array of shapes which turned out to be ships' propellers. Then down through tight tunnelling, and there you were. Packed into what today seems an improbably cramped site were sidings, the staithes themselves, an engine shed (sort of), and all the other kit needed to get coal from wagon into boat and away. Without the grandeur of Seaham, they had still shifted an awful lot of coal over the past century and more.

One afternoon at Sunderland Staithes I was offered 'a trip roond the bay' on an odd-looking, steam-powered vessel, brought temporarily back into action while its diesel replacement got repaired. The load? Yet more colliery waste. We stopped just past the breakwater; greasy black chains lifted the bottom doors and yet more stone and coal dust slipped into the filthy, churning seawater. Within twenty minutes we were tied up back at the staithes, the elderly vessel hissing softly, as if very, very tired.

Above and left: Advertising Roy Orbison's tour date in Sunderland. Maybe a contrast with Vernon, Texas?

Sunderland Station in the 1960s: a great deal of exhaust is coming from this Q6 freight engine—for no obvious reason, seeing that it isn't pulling anything. But a nice effect, and one you can't get from a diesel. Sunderland lacked the kind of direct express passenger service you might expect from the city of this size (although it wasn't difficult to change at Newcastle). The coast line had long-term subsidence problems, was built as a series of local lines rather than a through route—and there was always a feeling that freight came first.

NCB locomotives at Philadelphia: a substantial operation, fully the equal of a lot of BR freight sheds, but with endless character and variety.

NCB trains to Sunderland were run to mainline standards; they had to be because they ran over the main BR line to Durham on long-established running powers—but the NCB footplate men hadn't the company-issue boiler suits or grease-top hats of their BR counterparts. A thick coat and flat cap seem to have been the uniform of choice for skilled workers in many heavy industries for generations.

Much of the route involved running over modern, well maintained British Rail track with all the standard features you would expect. On the Coal Board's own network, things could be engagingly different.

A young visitor at Philadelphia.

A general view of Sunderland Staithes: the funnel of a vessel tied up; well-ordered strings of NCB Lambton wagons; shunters in attendance; the bridges and the river.

Above and opposite: South Dock.

The gear for getting the coal into the ships' holds, with the Wearmouth Bridge in the background (it has a freight train trundling across if you look closely).

Ready for a 'trip roond the bay,' delivering more colliery waste to the bottom of the North Sea.

The landward view as the waste met the waves; breakwater nearest, shipyards beyond. The moment the tipping took place was strangely undramatic: grey rocks shuffled away, to be replaced by churning black water.

I travelled to Sunderland in more conventional ways during the 1960s, but nothing stands out like a footplate trip.

As well as the shipbuilding, Sunderland was home to major employers in industries including glass-making and crane-building. Fundamental changes since then, of course. Large current employers like Nissan lay far in the future. Indeed what is now the university did not even become the polytechnic until 1969.

Throughout the area, many buildings—particularly those constructed in a hurry in the heady days of nineteenth-century growth—were not in good condition at all. In some places, the Luftwaffe had paved the way for comprehensive redevelopment, but then along came much more systematic, municipal programs for demolishing old buildings and replacing them with something more 'modern'. Councils could easily point to damp walls and the few amenities, often with significant health implications. In many respects, though, houses like these simply became unfashionable, and down they came.

Of course, we now know that the brave new concrete world has drawbacks too, and that comprehensive redevelopment can have delays and uncertainties which fracture communities and relationships. But at least initially, great hopes were pinned on redevelopment schemes, with the expectation that people would readily enough adopt the behavioural patterns which suited the new architecture best. Unfortunately, life turned out not to be quite like that and phrases like 'planning blight' came into general use, carried along by widespread speculation about what 'they' were going to deliver.

North Shields and South Shields face each other across the very last couple of miles before the Tyne reaches the North Sea. Interesting little ferries crossed the gap for most of the 1960s, but in 1967, a definite wonder of the local world was opened in the shape of tunnels for vehicles (a tunnel for pedestrians and cyclists had been open since 1951); a second pair of tunnels for vehicles was to open in 2011.

To me, North and South Shields always felt a bit different from the rest of Tyneside, probably because of their proximity to the sea, along with the width of the Tyne at that point, after its fairly constricted run between Newcastle and Gateshead. There were other differences, too: South Shields was an independent County Borough until 1974. In the 1960s, uniquely for the Tyne, Wear, and Tees, North Shields retained a sizeable fishing fleet.

Up the Tyne, both banks have seen quays and shipyards and housing developments over many generations, but there were still gaps—in the 1960s this included the strangely quiet and windswept Jarrow Slake. 'Reclamation' during the 1970s essentially swapped some flat, dry ground, suitable for parking cars going for export, for some flat, muddy tidal ground which was said to have been a good feeding ground for wading birds, although not of the sort to put on any kind of a show when I was there.

Anyway, it appears that this was once 'King Ecgfrith's Port', named after the Dark Age Northumbrian king who gifted the land to the monks of Jarrow. The wider area has deep, internationally important historical roots: the Venerable Bede worked here in the seventh and eighth centuries, at the closely linked churches of

In the North East, as in many other parts of Britain, terraced houses were making way for 'the future'.

Above and next page: The sometimes uncomfortable juxtaposition of old communities and shiny new replacements.

As time went on, things changed: much traditional housing ended up being retained and, eventually, improved. The experience of living in new estates on the edge of town, or high-rise flats closer in, did not always live up to the high-minded visionary expectations of planners and architects. Traditional scenes like these didn't seem so bad after all. The poster on the side of the shop promotes Sunderland *vs* Fulham at Roker Park: comfortable, familiar, somehow closer to the natural order of things for many people.

The North Shields fishing fleet, with South Shields beyond.

Above, below and opposite above: North Shields: very close to the North Sea.

Down to the quayside at North Shields.

Monkwearmouth and Jarrow. Facts like these had a definite aura to read about. Unfortunately I can't say that standing by the essentially mundane, estuarial Jarrow Slake in the 1960s brought back anything of these long-gone times. But the peace and relative tranquillity made it, for a while, a welcome break from the noisy modern world not so very far away.

Working out why I have fewer photographs of Tyneside and Wearside by comparison with Teesside is hardly difficult: I just didn't go there so often. I did go for a job interview at Reyrolles in Hebburn in 1965—thankfully these discerning people turned me down—and managed to take my camera with me, as well as returning later.

When I did get to Tyneside or Wearside, some interesting images were easy to spot; others needed working for. Let's first look at what many people would see as an icon of the Tyne and the Wear: the shipyard crane. There was no denying that the two rivers looked a bit different. Most of the land on lower Tyneside is fairly flat, so it was easy to see cranes stretching away into the distance from the right angle. In Sunderland, the river has cut its way down into a much tighter space with shorter perspectives.

As we have discussed earlier, the decline of the UK shipbuilding industry was no sudden, 1960s thing. Indeed Doxford's opened their new undercover Pallion shipyard as late as 1975, in what turned out to be largely a gesture towards international competitiveness in a battle which was essentially lost.

These forces underpin what was happening on the Tyne and the Wear. Although there is one big vessel building on a slipway over on the north bank of the Tyne, these images show few ships in any stage of construction or repair. And just as with pit village terraced houses put up in a hurry to house miners (pitmen, I mean), many of the houses for shipyard workers were no longer needed by their original work groups and became vulnerable to demolition and redevelopment.

But these were complicated times and the public mood held much more than gloom and doom (at least, that was what the papers said). From Newcastle City Hall came the voice of a man who seemed then to stand out as a genuine visionary. To some people he still does. Councillor T. Dan Smith was prone to refer to Newcastle as 'the Brasilia of the North', taking its cue from Barcelona and Manhattan rather than tired old British models or the dead hand of Whitehall. OK, he was sent to prison for six years as part of the Poulson corruption affair, but as I write this in 2015, with the airwaves ringing with talk of 'city regions' and 'economic powerhouses in the north', several commentators have brought up the memory of T. Dan Smith and I can understand why.

But this is a book of photographs, not political history, and I've a few more to include before the end.

To start with, there was and still is the elegant spire of St Andrew's Presbyterian Church in Hebburn, amid the rapidly diminishing stock of housing nearby. The building is a church no more, but that's still an imposing spire. A shipyard link comes from the man who largely funded the church's construction, Andrew Leslie—a major shipyard-owner, with the successor business, Hawthorn Leslie, still a significant employer in the 1960s.

Above and right: Jarrow Slake.
Considerable industrial and
commercial development close by
(including over the river). Relative
peace and quiet (then) in the
immediate area.

Above and left: Under the staithes at Jarrow. Business as usual: coal to load, crews to find, bills to pay.

Tyneside had more than shipbuilding and coal shifting: plenty of manufacturing took place on big sites and smaller ones tucked away.

The waves of demolition roll on through communities on the Durham bank. The famous name of 'Swan Hunter and Wigham Richardson' is apparent across the Tyne in Northumberland. There certainly were hopes that British shipbuilding could be revived. But nobody was able to work out how. It was like the thinking behind the tower blocks in the background which should have been the answer to many people's housing problems. But all too often, they weren't.

Above and below: Shipyards sat within communities as they always had, providing busy, noisy, well-paid work for the people who lived in the terraced housing nearby. I may well have taken these images on a weekend evening, but even so it's striking that so few people seem to be about. Bit by bit, the streets were getting quiet, mirroring the orders for the shipyards and the many other firms who supplied them. By the 1960s, a lot of the houses were under threat for failing to meet modern accommodation standards, and also because the dwindling number of shipyard workers needed dwindling numbers of houses.

Something big is on the slipway over on the north bank of the Tyne. But not many workers about, nor many ships, as Britain loses what was, for a long time, a world-leading industry.

The hammerhead crane is marked 'NEM' for the North Eastern Marine Engine Co., across the river in Wallsend.

Left and below: St Andrew's
Presbyterian Church, Hebburn;
traditional jobs going, traditional
homes going, traditional faith
under pressure.

Above and below: The bridges over the Tyne and nearby. Plenty of change here, of course, but several common factors: the river and bridges, inevitably, but also the climb needed to get from the quayside to the city centre. Incidentally, getting a warship built at Elswick—especially a big one—down to the sea must have been worth watching.

Another Tyne Bridge image, but the foreground has an interesting selection of British cars of the 1960s, whose designers have caught American influences and adopted tailfins.

To close this chapter, a brief return to the Penshaw Monument. I have no particular wish to glorify the Earl of Durham, but this image has only some exuberant foreground wild flowers in focus, the monument itself is blurred. (No, it wasn't an accident; with an Exakta you could do these sorts of things all those years ago.) Maybe it says something about change in this area: a proud but regimented past giving way to something more spontaneous and creative, if difficult to control or direct ... or maybe not. At least, the thought leads on to the final chapter of all.

Continuing on up the river, we're soon into the territory of the famous bridges, which might justifiably warrant a whole book on their own. I'd like to have been able to keep on going up to Dunston Staithes, in particular to compare this facility with similar structures at Seaham and Sunderland. The only thing is, while I visited Dunston in its working days on a couple of occasions, I never photographed the staithes until they were part of the Gateshead Garden Festival in 1990—just one of a large number of omissions I can do nothing about. But then again, there are only so many pages in a book like this, and it hasn't been difficult to fill them.

5
And Finally…

I suppose we all know what happened next—to coal mining and shipbuilding, to Roy Orbison and The Animals, but also to Nissan and the Sage Group. The 1960s in the North East of England were complex: they were 'swinging' for some, but their economic problems more seriously called for the appointment of a special cabinet minister.

Maybe that's enough analysis: not ignoring the economics and the perpetual challenges to the industrial base, I've chosen to end with a group of images which cut across the previous sections and show people from various parts of the area busily engaged at work, at play, and just sitting around mulling things over. Maybe they give a sense of particular times and particular places increasingly distant from the North East of today.

Above and below: Men at work on big industrial sites. Usually well-paid, often poor in long-term health implications, only very occasionally immediately dangerous—if you knew what you were doing.

Above and below: Men could easily be dwarfed by nature too: here a sea stack holds out against the pounding North Sea. Part of the black effect comes from taking the photograph against the sun; that wasn't the whole story in the 1960s, though, and a combination of coal waste being tipped into the sea and coal-derived air pollution meant that sightings of golden cliffs were rare.

Above, below and next two pages: Action at fairs around the region: not always easy to capture any image at all, let alone any evidence of all that noise, movement, and energy.

Above, below and next page: Whitby: visitors watch the sea, chat to each other, and press on with their knitting. Lifeboatmen just have a chat.

Above and opposite above: Roker.

Opposite below: A final look at floral Saltburn.

And to end both the chapter and the book, a cheery wave from Marsden rocks. On the Durham coast, not far from the mouth of the Tyne, this is the only place I can immediately think of where parking in a drab car park, then descending 100 feet in a lift leads to a fair-sized pub on the shoreline—protected, at least to some extent, by interesting sea stacks and arches. It looks as if the man in the dark coat is simply trying to attract the attention of friends or relatives. On the other hand, this place gets busy: he might just be trying to attract the waitress's attention about a missing plate of fish, chips, and mushy peas. I fear we will never know.

One example of comprehensive change occuring during the 1960s came on the railways. At the start of the decade, definitely in the steam age; by 1967–68, definitely not. Diesels and electric locomotives could go for much longer without maintenace, didn't need coal or firemen, and could point to other accountancy-friendly attributes. While not of themselves disastrous, the loss of well-paid jobs and yet more orders for coals didn't exactly reverse worrying economic trends.

Engineering know-how applied in very different settings: Saltburn pier and the coaling stage at Philadelphia, hub of an extensive private railway network operated by the NCB.

By way of contrast with the busy towns and cities and the sprawling industrial sites, the North East has varied and attractive countryside—beautiful in many different ways, yet sometimes overlooked by locals and visitors alike.

Endnotes

Introduction

1 British Rail after 1965.

4. Tyne and Wear

1 Lorenz, Edward H., *Towards a Theory of British Economic Decline: The Case of Shipbuilding, 1890–1970*, Kellogg Foundation Working Paper No. 148, November 1990 (ttp://kellogg.nd.edu/publications/workingpapers/WPS/148.pdf).
2 See Durham Mining Museum (www.dmm.org.uk).